DEAFINITIONS
For
SIGNLETS

Ken Glickman

Illustrated by Randy Lyhus

LICKED 'N' CLICKED   *(LIKT an KLIKT)*
adj. Feeling somewhat sheepish after futilely attempting
to make a selection on a vending machine only to find
the rejected coin in the "CHANGE" receptacle.

DEAFINITIONS
For
SIGNLETS*

*Any word pertaining to the world of the deaf
that isn't in the dictionary, but should be.

Published by **DiKen Products**
9201 Long Branch Parkway, Silver Spring, Maryland 20901

2-12-90   9,50   B+T

DEAFINITIONS For SIGNLETS
First Edition
Text by Ken Glickman
Illustrations by Randy Lyhus

Also by Ken Glickman
DEAFinitions, the poster
    Contains 50 humorous sentences - each using the word, deaf.
    Black on white, 100 lbs. quality gloss paper.
    Two sizes: 16'' by 20'' and 24'' by 36''

Copyright 1986 by Kenneth P. Glickman
Library of Congress Catalog Card Number: 86-72758
ISBN 0-9617583-0-9

Proudly printed in the United States of America

Dedicated

to

All 23 pairs of chromosomes
that lie inside all of us,
that dictate who we are.

Acknowledgements with Special Thanks

David W. Black
Catherine Burland
Diane and Dillip Emmanuel
Marie Emmanuel
Audrey and David Frank
Paula Hill
Pat Johanson
Robert Lewis
Carol I. Roberts
Michael W. Schuster
Marylynn Marrese Sullivan
Stephen W. Sullivan
Clare Tolan

And my family ... Dad, Mom, Tom, and Karen.

Table of Contents

A HEARIE's Foreword

It is only appropriate that this book of **SIGNLETS** has two forewords: one from the deaf perspective, the other from the hearing world. Both groups are addressed directly, and both groups will find humor here. In fact, much of the humor lies in the interaction between **DEAFIES** and **HEARIES**. The misunderstandings, conflicts, and everyday concerns that occur when the two worlds try to coexist and sometimes collide, makes for the very best stuff of humor. Through this humor, we see the world through each other's eyes - with all of its problems, frustrations, and, yes, hilarity.

Even those **SIGNLETS**, that have significance mainly to the deaf, are so wonderfully descriptive in this book that we can all relate to them. The humorous, and sometimes painful, situations that the deaf find themselves in, are delightfully captured in phrases that give voice to the deaf experience. They offer us a small glimpse into a world that many have ignored or were even embarrassed to enter.

The book's author is uniquely suited to navigate us between these two worlds, for he has lived and been a keen observer in both. From his undergraduate days as the only deaf student at Dartmouth College to his most recent position as a Visiting Professor under IBM Faculty Loan Program at Gallaudet University, Ken Glickman has often bridged the gap between the hearing and deaf worlds in ways that few people are able to do. Through humor or confrontation, with a magic trick or a provocative question, he has, for many years, given us **HEARIES** insight into the deaf world. In his humorous book of **SIGNLETS**, he shows us the most important lesson the deaf can teach: namely, being observant to the details of the world around us.

Michael W. Schuster, M.D.
Brookline, Massachusetts
Dartmouth '77

8

A DEAFIE's Foreword

As Ken remarks in his preface, language evolves by the birth and death of words. An incredible variety of people have contributed to English - Viking farmers, French lawyers, Afro-American musicians, baseball players, poets - and now, with this book, **DEAFIES**. They are lovely words, these **SIGNLETS** coined by Ken Glickman, wordsmith par excellence.

Let me demonstrate how useful and expressive they are by a brief description of two **PRENIKS** and their world. I start by taking my oath that Ken Glickman and I both are certifiably and not slightly but profoundly **DEAFORMED** ('deaf') and that we have been so all our lives.

To be more precise, I am a **HEAFIE**, or even possibly a **DEAFECTOR**, to the extent that I have tied the **INTER-EAR KNOT** with a very hearing **DEARIE**. Ken is a more rebellious **HEAFIE**: he is a **ZESTROLLING QUIETBUSTER** who undergoes **SCHIZOMORPHOSIS** daily and is dedicated to **MYTHICIDE** by **WITORTING** as well as to the abolition of **BERMUDEAF TRIANGLES**.

We attended Clarke School for the Deaf, which is dedicated to molding **DEAFIES** into **FAR-LIPPED DEAFEATISTS** rather than **OVERASLAPPING DEAFIANTISTS**. We **SITRAIGHTINED** and **COMFRONTED** each other prior to **EXAGGERTICULATING PAC-MANESE**, although we often **ACCELEPRATED** or **OOGLATAKOOPED**. We always **COMMUNAVIGATED**, **RADARSCANNING** for **DANCETAPPERS** and **OOPSTACLES**. And we **ATTENTAPPED**, **BIPEDATTENTAPPED**, and **TABLE-TAPPED** each other constantly, until we suffered from **TAPCRATERS** and **STOMPOPHOBIA**. We **EYESDROPPED** on each other, **AFFIRMINKLED** in agreement and **TONEWALLED** in disagreement. We abused our hearing aids, which we **BEEPPLUGGED**, **PICKROLLFLICKED**, and **PSEUDOKNOBBED**.

9

Our teachers were trained to use the **LITEMUS-TEST**, to avoid **TAUTLIPS**, and to deal with **MARBLOCUTIONS** and **PHIPHTHEENS**. They as well as our families at home continually endured **DRIPTORTURE**, **DINNER-DIN**, **CACOINPHONY**, **WUNNING**, and **PEDODRAG** from us, while in the outside world, we put up with **BACKTALKERS**, **GLASSHOLES**, and **HEYBARKERS**.

If the reader will take the trouble to look up the **DEAFINITIONS** of the **SIGNLETS** used above, he will see that the previous three paragraphs describe a range of **DEAFIE** phenomena and situations which would require several pages to translate into ordinary **HEARIE** English. Ken's school days are long behind him; he went on to battle **GAWKWARD**, **DEAFEARING**, and **DEAFACED HEARIES** and the hated **BERMUDEAF TRIANGLES** in his subsequent experiences as a college student and an IBM programmer. He has travelled in Europe and has taught at Rochester and Gallaudet, where he encountered **EGOPRETERS**, **SIGNORAMUSES**, and **SYGNOPHANTS**. This book is merely a preliminary distillation of that rich experience.

This is a **DEAFIE** work of visual humor. Close your ears as you read it. And laugh as noisily as you please.

Stephen W. Sullivan
Bay Shore, Long Island
Yale '77

Playing It by Eye

There exists within the vast world of the hearing, a much smaller world of the deaf. It is from this sometimes noisy deaf world that I hope to bring some insight to those who can hear, and good-natured chuckles to those who can't.

In this unmistakably unique world of the deaf, light "speaks louder" than sound, and sign language communicates more swiftly and eloquently than the spoken word as attested by the adage: "A picture is worth a thousand words." Almost all, if not all, acoustical systems in the hearing world have their counterparts in the world of the deaf: lights flash on and off whenever a phone or a door bell rings; phones are answered via telecommunication devices for the deaf (TDDs), by which the deaf "talk" by typing; TV shows are understood via telecaptions. It is, in short, a visual-oriented world.

The inhabitants of this small world are a remarkably enterprising people. With one less sense than the hearing's five senses, this "silent" minority can do everything the hearing do...even "listening" by sight. **DEAFIES**, as they are referred to in this book, are found in every nook and cranny of the hearing world. Often, they are incredibly hard to detect: they look, eat, work, play, and even make love just like the **HEARIES**.

However, it is in the area of communication that a major difference lies between these two "species" of Homo sapiens. **HEARIES**, due to evolutionary chance, far outnumber **DEAFIES**, and the spoken word thus prevails over the signed gesture. **DEAFIES** are born into the hearing world and are thus faced with the great challenge of mastering the **HEARIES'** horrendously complex language—with all her intonations, inflections, silent consonants, double entendres, and idiomatic expressions. Some **DEAFIES** are raised as manualists, using only sign language, while some others are painstakingly taught to speak vocally and to read lips—the so-called oralists. A great many **DEAFIES** fall somewhere in between the two worlds.

11

Since communication is undoubtedly a crucial factor in determining who "flocks" with whom, and since it is also often the comical, if not sad, reason for so many misunderstandings between the two worlds, it is therefore hoped that this book will contribute towards bridging this communication gap in some small way.

Many situations encountered by **DEAFIES** and **HEARIES** alike have (until now) defied description. This book is intended to rescue those of us who have experienced such situations but have been at a loss to express them succinctly and vividly. In response to this loss for words, new words have been invented and are listed herein. They are affectionately called **SIGNLETS**, and their **DEAFINITIONS** sometimes contain **SIGNLETS** (always in bold-face for easy identification).

Also, it can serve as a reference for those of us who, having experienced a particular situation, want to know whether there is an English word or phrase for it. Since it is impossible to list situations in some kind of order, it is recommended that this book be read in its entirety to determine whether the situation has been accounted for. If not, then you as the reader have a golden opportunity to contribute to the evolving English language!

Like any language, English is an evolving language. Words get born, take on color with maturity, and sometimes simply fade into oblivion. Thoughts, ideas, concepts, experiences, and observations spring up here and there—in the minds of all of us—seen or unseen, experienced or unexperienced, and most of all, captured or uncaptured on paper. Just as evolution testifies to the premise of the survival of the fittest, may this book then be a testimony to the survival of the most appropiate word or phrase!

Ken Glickman
Silver Spring, Maryland
October 1, 1986

SIGNLETS

AAAHOOO

(AAAAAAAH HOOOOOOO)

n. The morning ritual in which **DEAFIES** test batteries in their hearing aids by cooing to themselves.

ACCELEPRATE
(ak SEL uh prayt)

v. To chatter at an increasingly incoherent speed.

AFFIRMINKLES
(af FIR ming kuls)

n. Cute wrinkles that form around a **DEAFIE**'s nose from the habit of wriggling it in affirmation.

ALPHABUM
(al fuh BUM)

n. Deaf "ABC" card peddler.

AMBULOPHOBIA
(AM byuh luh FOH bee uh)

n. The fear of entering a traffic intersection unaware of the approach of an ambulance, a firetruck, or a police car with wailing sirens.

ANATHEMOSIS
(AN a the MOH sis)

n. A writing disorder, affecting many **DEAFIES**, in which the articles (an, a, the) are often mixed up.

ANPERPLEXIOUS
(an per PLEK shus)

adj. Stumped at a locked restroom door at a restaurant, not knowing whether to knock or to ask for the key.

AQUARANTINE
(ak WA run teen)

n. A system often employed by **DEAFIES** where all the faucets in the house are manually and visually inspected for **WUNNING** before going to bed or leaving on vacation.

AQUASHOCK
(ak wa SHOK)

n. The utterly helpless feeling deaf divers experience when they suddenly realize (in midair) that they have a hearing aid on.

ARMED ZONE
(armd zohn)

n. Dangerous area around manual **DEAFIES**, especially for non-spectacled bystanders.

17

ASLIGN
(AY es el YN)

v. To align oneself in a comfortable position before using American Sign Language (ASL).

ASSENSE
(AS sens)

n. The ability, possessed by **DEAFIES**, of feeling vibrations (such as those coming from an airplane flying overhead) in the seat of their pants.

ATTENTAP
(uh TEN tap)

v. To touch the arm or shoulder of a **DEAFIE** prior to speaking and/or signing.

18

ATTITUTUNE
(AT uh tew tewn)

v. 1. To alter his communication style when a **DEAFIE** realizes the listener is not deaf. 2. To come to realization of **DEAFIES'** capabilities and accomplishments.

AUDIBORETORIUM
(aw di BOR ah tawr ee um)

n. The sea of signing hands in any bored deaf audience.

AUTOMOBABBLE
(AW tuh moh BAB bel)

v. To huddle and chat by the night light inside a car (while driving at night).

BACKTALK

(BAK tawk)

v. To lecture, while writing on the blackboard, a **HEARIE** class with at least one **DEAFIE** student.

BATTER-WEAK

(BAT ur week)

n. The lifespan of the battery in a hearing-aid before it sputters and dies.

BEEPPLUG

(BEEP plug)

v. To press the hearing-aid earmold deeper into the ear in the hope of stopping whistling sounds.

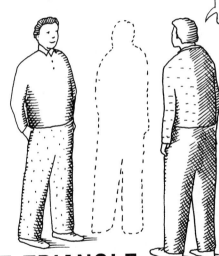

BERMUDEAF TRIANGLE

(ber MEW def TRY ang gul)

n. A communication situation where the **DEAFIE** "disappears" once a second **HEARIE** joins the conversation between him and the first **HEARIE**.

BICULTUREOUS
(BY KUL chur ee us)

adj. Inclined to go back and forth between **DEAFIE** and **HEARIE** worlds.

BIPEDATTENTAP
(BY ped uh TEN tap)

v. To try, often as a last resort, to get a **DEAFIE**'s attention by stomping with two feet.

BLITTIES

BLESSIC
(BLES sik)

adj. Feeling incredibly smug when one works noisily in the knowledge his/her spouse is totally deaf.

BLITTIES
(BLIT eez)

n. Hardened blisters only found on finger tips and the outward sides of thumbs. Attributed to the heavy use of older teletypes (TTYs) with manual keyboards.

BOOBAPPARITION

(BOOB ap uh RISH un)

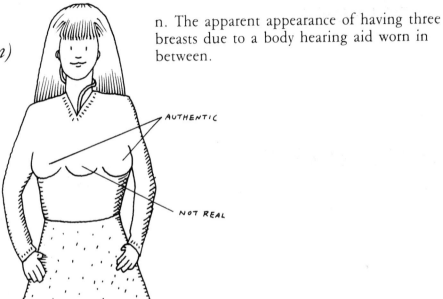

n. The apparent appearance of having three breasts due to a body hearing aid worn in between.

AUTHENTIC

NOT REAL

BOREDLIKEHELLUS

(bohrd lyk HELL us)

n. A minor ailment, very much like a common cold, where there is a sore red spot on the right side of the victim's nose. Attributed to the chronic pressure of the right index finger in the actual sign for "boring".

BULBSESSION
(bulb SESH un)

n. An abnormal mental disorder in which a **DEAFIE** repeatedly checks all the phone and doorbell light bulbs to see if they are in place and working properly.

BYEXAGGERATION
(BY eg zaj uh RAY shun)

n. The long-winded ritual found almost exclusively among **DEAFIES** in which visitors and hosts may take two hours to reach the front door from the kitchen, punctuated by ''I have to go right now'' and ''You have to go right now''.

CABOOSED
(kuh BOOSD)

adj. Being the last to know about the latest rumor. (Used especially for **DEAFIES** in a hearing environment.)

CACOINPHONY
(ka KOYN fuh nee)

n. Discordant sounds arising from the monetary change in the pockets of a walking **DEAFIE**.

CADAVERPRETING
(kuh DAV er pruht ing)

v. Interpreting with a poker face.

CAFFEINT
(kaf FAYNT)

v. To pretend to laugh during coffee breaks (in hearing companies).

CAMOUFLAGISM
(KAM uh flazh iz um)

n. A theory that explains how some **DEAFIES** are able to fool **HEARIES** by passing as foreigners.

25

CATCHAJERK
(KAT cha jerk)

n. Any muscular movement that unintentionally draws attention from a **DEAFIE**.

CHAOTICHARCOAL
(kay OT i CHAR kohl)

n. Burned popcorn in a **DEAFIE**'s kitchen.

CHINSLAP
(chin SLAP)

n. An embarrassing situation where a male interpreter accidently flips his tie onto his face.

CIRCUMSIGNUTION
(SIR kum syn OO shun)

n. Evasive signs used by deaf politicians when confronted with direct questions.

27

CLANKOUSTICS
(klank KOO stiks)

n. The science of the sounds created by **DEAFIES** eating with forks and knives on china plates.

CLARKE-BARK
(KLARK-BARK)

v. To **COMFRONT** an oralist and demand whether he went to Clarke School for the Deaf.

CLASSIC CLASSROOM CLASHING
(KLAS ik   KLAS room   KLASH ing)

n. The perplexing condition a **DEAFIE** often finds himself in, where the professor, the interpreter, and the notetaker all appear to be saying different things simultaneously.

COMFRONT
(kom FRUNT)

v. To turn to face a **DEAFIE** before speaking.

COMMUNAVIGATE
(kuh mew NAV uh gayt)

v. To find one's way through a herd of **DEAFIES** without crossing any **VISUALINES** of communication.

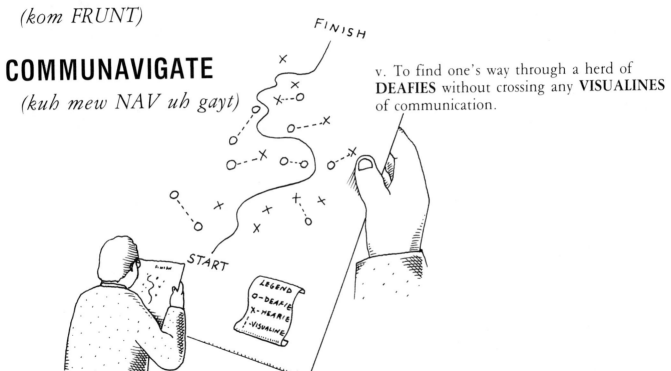

29

CONDUCTORF
(kun DUK torf)

v. To wake up traveling **DEAFIES** at their destinations. (A note of interest: **DEAFIES** are notorious for sleeping through anything and everything.)

CONTACTFUL
(kun TAKT ful)

adj. Courteous in **ATTENTAPPING**.

COOKITCHAT
(koo KIT chat)

v. To make some small talk compulsively only in the brightly lit kitchen.

COUNTER ENCOUNTER JITTERS
(KOWN tur en KOWN tur JIT erz)

n. Nervous apprehension some **DEAFIES** experience at a crowded counter in a noisy store, unsure on whether or not to wait until all other customers have left before addressing the salesperson.

CRANECK

(krayn NEK)

v. To ignore the cashier's lips and to crane one's neck to see the total price on the cash register.

D.D.D.'s (Damn Deafie Drivers)
(DEE DEE DEEZ)

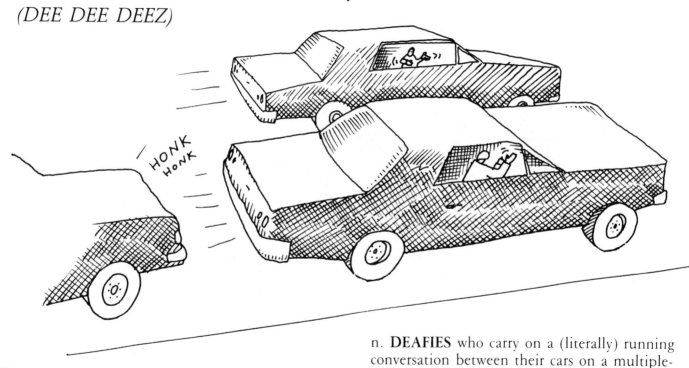

n. **DEAFIES** who carry on a (literally) running conversation between their cars on a multiple-lane highway.

DANCEDUNCE
(DANS DUNS)

n. A **DEAFIE** dancing to a blaring radio that is all news and no music.

DANCETAP
(DANZ tap)

v. To jump up and down and wave one's arms in front of a **DEAFIE** to catch his attention.

DARF SIDE
(darf syd)

n. The ''blind'' spot behind a **DEAFIE**'s back that moves every time he **RADARSCANS**.

DEAF DATE
(def dayt)

n. Someone whom you never hear from again.

DEAF NOSE
(def nohs)

n. Clogged-up proboscis. (Not as in "Deaf knows.")

DEAF POWER
(def POW ur)

n. A defiant protest where a **DEAFIE** covers one ear with one hand and raises the other in a fist. (Not to be confused with the Black Power gesture.)

DEAF-IMPAIRED
(DEF im PAYRD)

n. Anyone who is not hearing-impaired; a **HEARIE**.

DEAFACEMENT

(dee FAYS ment)

n. Anything that impedes face-to-face communication with **DEAFIES**, such as a moustache, a smoking pipe, a pair of dark sunglasses, nervous head movements, or a big red pimple.

DEAFAME
(de FAYM)

n. Deaf gossip.

DEAFEAR
(def FEER)

n. An acute phobia among **HEARIES** who always respond with "Oh!" or "YES!?" when, to their terror, they are addressed by a **DEAFIE**.

DEAFEATIST
(def EET ist)

n. A **DEAFIE** who refuses to learn sign language.

DEAFECTOR
(de FEK tur)

n. A **DEAFIE** who no longer socializes with other **DEAFIES**.

DEAFECTS
(de FEKTS)

n. Hearing parents with deaf kids. (Compare with **DEAFUNCTS**.)

DEAFENDER
(de FEND er)

n. Any active member of the National Association of the Deaf (NAD).

DEAFENING
(DEF un ing)

n. A court hearing in the deaf world.

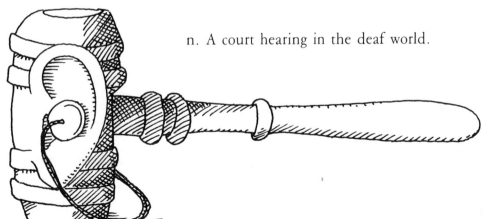

DEAFENSE MECHANISM
(de FENS   MEK uh niz um)

n. (Psychological jargon) A type of reaction, in which a **DEAFIE** puts blame for failure on his deafness instead of on his own shortcomings.

DEAFERENCE THEORY
(DEF uh ruhns   THEE uh ree)

n. A theory which explains why some **DEAFIES** often allow themselves to be brainwashed by **HEARIES**.

DEAFFISHING
(def FISH ing)

n. A road game where players take turns in the nighttime trying to find **DEAFIES** whose car's auxiliary lights are on in the moving sea of cars.

DEAFIANTIST
(de FY un tist)

n. A **DEAFIE** who refuses to speak.

DEAFICIENT
(de FISH unt)

adj. 1. Lacking in experience with or knowledge of the deaf and deafness. 2. Not feeling comfortable as a deaf individual.

DEAFIE
(DEF ee)

n. A deaf person who acts and looks like one.

DEAFIE'S DELIGHT
(DEF eez di LYT)

n. A real cheap house right next to a busy interstate road or airport.

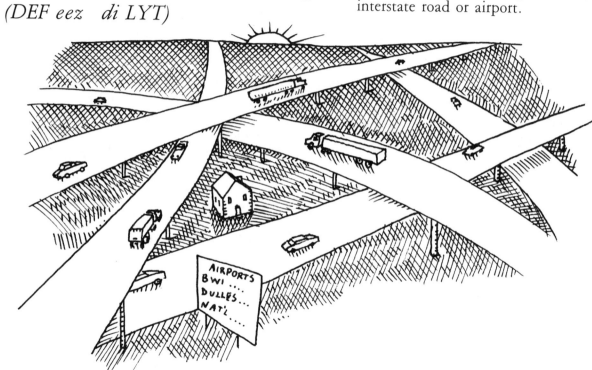

DEAFINITIONS

(def uh NISH unz)

n. Definitions of **SIGNLETS**.

DEAFLATEDLORY

(de FLAYT ed lor ee)

adj. Feeling real sheepish, such as after a 80-yard touchdown run only to learn the whistle has been blown 50 yards back.

DEAFLE-EYED

(def el YD)

adj. Possessing an uncanny ability to read lips across an immense distance, such as a football field.

DEAFLECTING
(de FLEKT ing)

v. Driving, signing, and swerving simultaneously by deaf drivers.

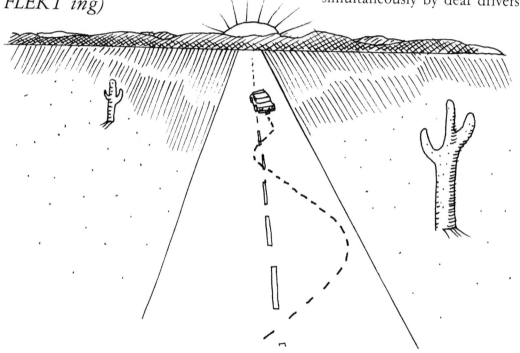

DEAFLY BIRD
(DEF lee BIRD)

n. A **DEAFIE** who tends to arrive early at gatherings since he wasn't sure whether it was fifteen or fifty minutes after the hour. (See **PHIPHTHEENS**.)

DEAFNOSTIC
(def NOS tik)

n. A **DEAFIE** who doubts the existence of his handicap.

DEAFORMED
(def ORMD)

adj. 1. Born deaf. 2. Being deaf.

DEAFRAUDS
(def RAWDZ)

n. Deaf parents with at least 12 damn hearing kids and no deaf kids.

DEAFUNCTS
(def UNKTS)

n. Deaf parents without deaf kids. (Compare with **DEAFECTS**.)

DEAFUSE
(de FEWS)

v. To convert an oral **DEAFIE** to the ways of the deaf world.

DEARIE
(DE ur ee)

n. A **HEARIE** who acts and looks like a **DEAFIE**.

DECAPTIONED
(de KAP shund)

adj. The sudden feeling of frustration a **DEAFIE** experiences when the TV movie he has been watching quickly looses its telecaptions in the last 15 climactic minutes.

DETOUR TAPE

(DEE toor   tayp)

n. The duct tape patched over the house doorbell of a **DEAFIE**'s home (often accompanied by a note saying: ''Please press the other button'').

DIMTALK
(dim TAWK)

v. To **EXAGGERTICULATE** slowly in any semi-darkened place.

DINNER-DIN
(DIN er DIN)

n. Irritable munching noises often emitted by deaf diners.

DOGEARCRATCH
(DOG eer KRATCH)

v. To shake the earmold to relieve the itching inside the ear.

DOTHS
(doths)

n. **DEAFIES** with the nocturnal habit of flocking toward and hanging around a 120-watt light bulb for hours at a stretch.

DRAP
(drap)

n. Any **DEAFIE** found locked inside a shop or library after the closing time due to not hearing the public announcement of impending closing.

DRIPTORTURE
(drip TOR chur)

n. The maddening state a **HEARIE** finds himself in after a **DEAFIE** leaves a faucet slightly open.

DRIVE-UPROAR
(DRYV up ROHR)

n. Momentary confusion at a Drive-Thru fast-food place that ensues when a deaf driver ignores the microphone/speaker apparatus and suddenly shows his face at the Drive-Up window.

DURP
(durp)

n. A loud burp emitted by a **DEAFIE**.

EARICAP
(EER ee kap)

n. The disadvantage that **HEARIES** experience in noisy places.

EARSNIFFING
(EER snif ing)

v. Checking behind another's ears to see if there is a hearing aid.

EGOPRETER
(ee GOH prit er)

n. An interpreter who puts on a great show.

ELECTROTRACKS
(i LEK truh TRAKS)

n. A trail of electric household appliances left running by deaf kids.

ELEVEQUILIBRIUM

(el uh VAY kwuh LIB ree um)

n. That particular spot in the hallway from where one can see all the elevators' lights without turning.

51

EMPATHECSTASY

(EM puh THEK stuh see)

n. An overpowering emotion experienced by **HEAFIES** induced by the realization that the person they thought was a **HEARIE** is actually a **HEAFIE** like themselves.

ENGLISHAME

(ENG gli shaym)

n. What often prevents **DEAFIES** from writing letters or making TDD phone calls or even buying this book.

ENRAPTIONED

(en RAP shund)

adj. Obsessively engrossed in watching close-captioned TV.

EXAGGERTICULATE

(eg ZAJ er TIK ew layt)

v. To speak in **PAC-MANESE**. (Often applied to **HEARIES** and oral **DEAFIES**.)

EXAMFLASH

(eg ZAM FLASH)

n. A subgroup of false fire alarms which occur mainly in classroom buildings where a difficult test is about to be given.

EXCHANGLE

(eks CHANG gel)

v. To switch seats with a **HEARIE** to obtain a better angle on lips and signs.

EXTEGRATION

(eks stuh GRAY shun)

n. A party-time phenomenon where both **HEARIES** and **DEAFIES** tend to flock as separate "birds of an ear."

EYESDROP
(YZ drop)

v. To read lips or signs without getting caught.

EYESOGRE
(YZ oh gur)

n. That hulking guy sitting in front of a **DEAFIE** and obstructing his view of the interpreter.

FACUS
(FAY kus)

n. That elusive focal point on a speaker's face on which a **DEAFIE** concentrates; it is known to blur out occasionally or to drift elsewhere.

FAR-LIPPED
(far lipt)

adj. (Same as **DEAFLE-EYED**.)

FINGRUNCH
(fing GRUNCH)

v. To type on a very small TDD keyboard.

FLARTULOUD
(f(l)ar too LOWD)

v. To emit gas unwittingly in public places.

FLASH-O-HOUSERN
(FLASH oh HOWS urn)

n. A **DEAFIE**'s house with a malfunctioning telephone/doorbell light system, which flickers through the night.

FLASHWALK

(FLASH wawk)

v. To reach a **DEAFIE**'s ringing telephone in the nighttime by walking during its flashes and pausing in between rings when it is utterly pitch black.

FLICKERCHAT
(flik er CHAT)

v. To converse by candlelight on a windy night.

FLOWER-REARRANGE
(FLOW er ree uh RAYNJ)

v. To move an obstructing centerpiece off to one side of the table prior to conversing.

57

FORTY-SEVEN DEGREE MODE

(FORT ee SEV un di GREE MOHD)

n. The communication method in which a deaf driver converses with a back-seat passenger via the rear-view mirror.

FOSSILLOTES
(FOS ul lohts)

n. Old scribbled notes found buried in coat pockets usually after a shopping trip.

FREEZING-MOLD
(FREEZ ing mold)

n. The action of keeping oneself absolutely immobile while a new hearing-aid earmold hardens in the ear.

FRUSTONE
(FRUS tohn)

n. Any alien sound not recognized by the teletype.

GALNTIDETIANS
(gal NID e tee ans)

n. Students known for their propensity for transfering back and forth between the two major colleges for the deaf.

GASK
(gask)

v. To ask the person on the other end of the telephone line bluntly if he is paying attention to the TDD's display and to sign off abruptly if there's no response.

GAWKWARD
(GAWK ward)

n. A brief encounter between a **DEAFIE** and a **HEARIE**, in which the **HEARIE** stammers ''Very nice to meet you'' and walks away.

GETTAPATTEN
(get TAP uh TEN)

v. To get a **DEAFIE**'s attention from a distance by enlisting a third person to **ATTENTAP** him.

GIGGLOPARANOID

(GIG loh PAR ah noyd)

adj. How a **DEAFIE** feels in a group of people when everyone laughs except him.

GLASSHOLE

(GLAS hohl)

n. A person who habitually talks to **DEAFIES** with his back to a brightly lit window.

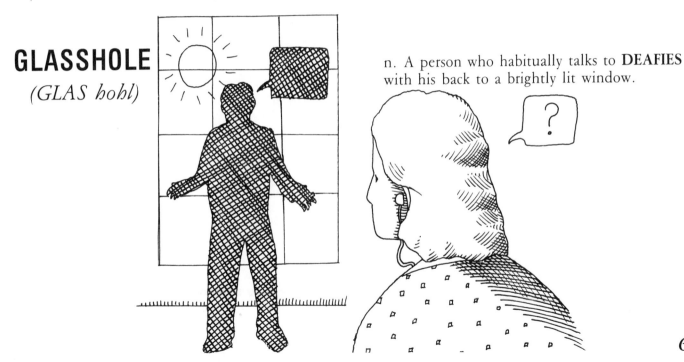

GLOBULARIZE
(GLOB ew lah ryz)

v. To cluster with other **DEAFIES** of a similar background, such as oralists, manualists, or **TOTALISTS**.

GLUEXCESSION
(glew ek SESH un)

n. Abnormal compulsion to watch TV, even the non-captioned commercials.

GRIPLINES
(grip lynz)

n. The tiny linear bumps on the volume knobs of hearing-aids.

HARD-OF-DEAF
(HARD of def)

adj. Unable to perceive most sounds. (Compare with **SOFT-OF-DEAF**.)

HEAFIE
(HEF ee)

n. A **DEAFIE** who acts and looks like a **HEARIE**.

HEARIE
(HEER ee)

n. One who hears most, if not all, of the ordinary sounds; **DEAF-IMPAIRED**.

HEARING AND DUMB
(HEER ing and DUM)

adj. A term that best describes **HEARIES** who keep referring to **DEAFIES** as "deaf and dumb".

HEARRING

(HEER ring)

n. The ear hearing-aid that has slipped out from behind the ear and is hanging down.

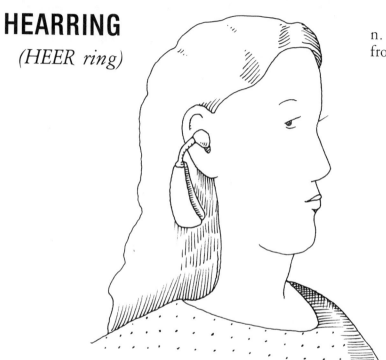

HEYBARK

(hey BARK)

v. To call after a **DEAFIE** who keeps walking away.

HUBBUBBLE
(hub BUB bul)

n. A loose, noisy pebble caught in the hubcap of a **DEAFIE**'s car.

HUMORIBUND
(hew MOR i bund)

v. To try to convince a **DEAFIE** that the joke he just missed wasn't that funny anyway.

HYBREED
(HY breed)

v. To mate and produce **SOFT-OF-DEAF** and/or **HARD-OF-DEAF** kids.

ID-DEMAND
(YD dee MAND)

v. To ask a stranger whether he is deaf or not.

IDIOT'S CONFIDANTE

(ID ee uts   KON fee dant)

n. A **DEAFIE** into whose ear one speaks earnestly.

IDIOT'S NOD

(ID ee uts   nod)

n. The blank look on a **HEARIE**'s face as he continues smiling and nodding when a **DEAFIE** has just finished asking him a question. Or, vice versa.

IDIOTSPRAY
(ID ee ut spray)

v. To talk loudly to a **DEAFIE** who isn't wearing any hearing aid (or even when he is), often characterized by **SPROXIMITES**.

INSCRIBBACK
(in SKRYB bak)

v. To spell on a **DEAFIE**'s back - usually during love-making. (See **LOVESPELL**.)

INSULTRUCTIONS
(in sul TRUK shuns)

n. 1. Instructions found in hearing aid packages that explain in kindergarten terms how to remove the old batteries, how to insert the new ones, and how to buy some more. 2. Obvious tips and explanations, imparted by **HEARIES**.

INTER-EAR KNOT
(IN ter EER NOT)

n. Marriage between a **DEAFIE** and a **DEARIE** (or between a **HEAFIE** and a **HEARIE**).

INTER-PAUSE
(IN ter PAWZ)

n. That very short disruption in a lecture that takes place once every thirty minutes when two interpreters exchange places.

INTERPRIVY
(IN ter PRIV ee)

n. A private conversation between an interpreter and a lone deaf client especially during a boring lecture. (See **SYNCHECK**.)

INVISIBLAME
(in VIZ i blaym)

v. To shout loudly at one's hearing child in the next room to stop fighting with his deaf brother (who is naturally delighted by the situation).

JETSTARTING
(JET start ing)

v. Trying to start a car when it's already running.

JINXOES
(jinks ohz)

n. The white boxes often found in garbled TV captions.

KESTUK
(KEE stuk)

n. A stuck key in the TDD keyboard.

69

LENS-PROPELMENT
(LENZ pruh PEL ment)

n. The sudden act of hurling one's glasses accidently while signing.

LICKED 'N' CLICKED
(LIKT an KLIKT)

adj. Feeling somewhat sheepish after futilely attempting to make a selection on a vending machine only to find the rejected coin in the "CHANGE" receptacle.

LIGHT-BULBED
(LYT bulbd)

adj. Being in the proximity of a 75-watt light bulb with one's back to it.

LIGHTGLOW
(LYT gloh)

n. Light rays coming out from behind the head of one who's **LIGHT-BULBED**. (Not to be confused with those from a saint's halo.)

LINGEROIDS
(LING ger oydz)

n. Several **DEAFIES** usually found staying on and chatting after a room is cleared of **HEARIES**.

LITEMUS-TEST
(LYT mus test)

v. To ask a deaf listener: ''Can you see me alright?''

LOVESPELL
(LUV spel)

v. To spell out by fingerspelling underneath the deaf lover's fingers in total darkness. (Note: this method of communication is used when it is not possible to **INSCRIBBACK**.)

MACHPRESSING
(mach PRES ing)

v. (Audiological jargon) Pressing the Tone button as if it were a machine gun. (Not to be confused with pumping the accelerator with the idea of reaching the speed of sound.)

MAGNETALK
(MAG ni TAWK)

v. To sign and kiss alternately.

MARBLOCUTIONS
(MAR bloh kew shuns)

n. Words mispronounced by **DEAFIES** (and sometimes **HEARIES**).

MASSESSMENT

(MAS es ment)

n. The process of trying to figure out what the hell is going on when there is a stampede of a million **HEARIES** running away from or toward something.

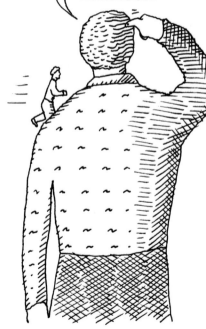

MINORSTREAM

(MY nor streem)

v. To mainstream deaf kids in hearing schools until the age of 16.

MIRROBERRATION

(MIR ob uh RAY shun)

n. An compulsive tendency to glance at the rearview and side mirrors repeatedly while driving. Often found in conjunction with **AMBULOPHOBIA**.

MMMEEENNNOOOMMM

(MMMMMM EEEEE NNNNNN OOOOOO MMMMM)

n. A highly specialized speech-training technique in which both the teacher and the student touch each other's nose and throat with their hands and drone out sounds.

MOLDWAXUS
(mold WAKS us)

n. The brownish wax found in the crevices of earmolds, usually removed by **WAXBLOWING**.

MONKEY'S ELBOW
(MUNG keez EL boh)

n. Awkwardness in signing.

MORNING ITCH
(MOR ning ICH)

n. An irritable ailment that often afflicts **DEAFIES** late in the evening, when an uncaptioned TV news flash arouses their curiosity and they can't wait to read about it in the morning paper.

MYTHICIDE
(MYTH i syd)

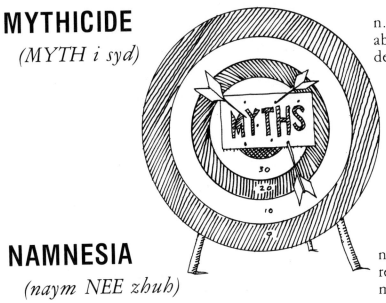

n. The act of educating the **DEAF-IMPAIRED** about the misconceptions and myths about deafness and the deaf.

NAMNESIA
(naym NEE zhuh)

n. The inability among many **DEAFIES** to recall the name of a person they've known for months.

NARCOLEPSIGN
(NAR koh LEP syn)

v. To communicate in sign language while asleep.

77

NCIOIDS
(NSEE oydz)

n. English-like words in garbled TV captions that require **DEAFIES** to decipher their significance. Examples: "LOST AND LESS" signifies "LOS ANGELES" and "ADD VERY TIES" signifies "ADVERTISE".

NEAR-LIPPED
(NEER lipt)

adj. Reading lips cross-eyed.

NITWHIT
(NIT whit)

n. A person who does not even realize his hearing aid is whistling.

NO-MOLD ZONE
(noh MOLD zohn)

n. The area in the ear channel between the eardrum and the end of the earmold, where wax accumulates and is **PICKROLLFLICKED**.

OGLETITIS
(og le TYT uhs)

n. The disgusting feeling that sets in after **RIPOSTARING**.

OOGLATAKOOP
(OOG la ta KOOP)

v. To talk less intelligibly due to embarrassment or shock.

OOPSNOTIC
(OOPS noh tik)

adj. Being somewhat flustered upon realizing the person a **DEAFIE** thought was **DANCETAPPING** at him was not trying for his attention.

OOPSTACLE
(OOPS stuh kul)

n. Anything that a walking **DEAFIE** bumps into, especially when deep in **RETRO-STROLLING** with another person.

OPHTHALMATIGUE
(of THAL mah teeg)

n. Eye strain from lipreading.

ORIENTOLAPSE
(OR ee ent oh laps)

n. The brief period of time following flashing alarm lights during which a **DEAFIE** is momentarily confused and tries to determine whether it is from the telephone or the door.

OSIGNCILLATE
(oh SYN si layt)

v. To emphasize one sign by shaking it rapidly back and forth as in the sign ''finish''!

OSTRACISMOTITIS
(os TRA kiz moh TYT uhs)

n. The feeling of bewilderment that sets in after being ''stoned'' by **HEARIES**.

OSTRICHEARIE
(AS trich HEER ee)

n. A **HEARIE** who pretends that there is no **DEAFIE** in a group when there is actually one on each side.

OVERASLAP
(OH ver AY es el ap)

n. The area between two signing **DEAFIES** where their hands collide.

PAC-MANESE
(PAK man EEZ)

n. The speech used by oral **DEAFIES**, characterized by **EXAGGERTICULATION**.

PACHYDACTYLOLOGY
(PAK i DAK ti LOH loh gee)

n. The study of people who are thick at learning sign language.

PARALYZOPTICALAPSE

(PAR ah lyz OP tik kal aps)

n. An impasse in a conversation which occurs when the **DEAFIE** automatically stops talking because the **HEARIE** looked away, breaking their eye contact.

PARASSITOLOGY

(PAR as sy TOH loh gee)

n. The scientific study of **DEAFIES** who survive solely on Social Security Income (SSI) in the hearing world.

PARKING BLUES

(PARK ing   blews)

n. The feeling **DEAFIES** often experience after deciding not to park in spaces designated by the blue signs for "HANDICAPPED ONLY".

PASS 'N' SIGN
(pas an syn)

n. A strategy borrowed from football, in which two walking **DEAFIES** keep tossing each other all their books so they can sign with free hands.

PEDODRAG
(PED oh drag)

n. (Aeronautical jargon) The force that acts on **DEAFIES'** feet in the opposite direction of their heading - causing sounds annoying to **HEARIES**.

PHIPHTHEEN
(fif THEEN)

n. Any troublesome word often mislipread by **DEAFIES**.

PHONYPHONICS
(FOH ne FOH niks)

n. **DEAFIES** with cochlear implants.

PICKROLLFLICK
(PIK rol flik)

v. To pick excess wax from the **NO-MOLD ZONE** inside the ear with one's fingernail, roll it in the fingers, and dispose of it by flicking.

PITCH PITS
(PICH pits)

n. The bottommost points on the red and blue curves on audiological charts that determine whether one has normal or abnormal hearing.

POINTOSPHERE
(POYNT oh sfeer)

n. The part of the sky **DEAFIES** point to when talking about people and/or places not within their immediate sight.

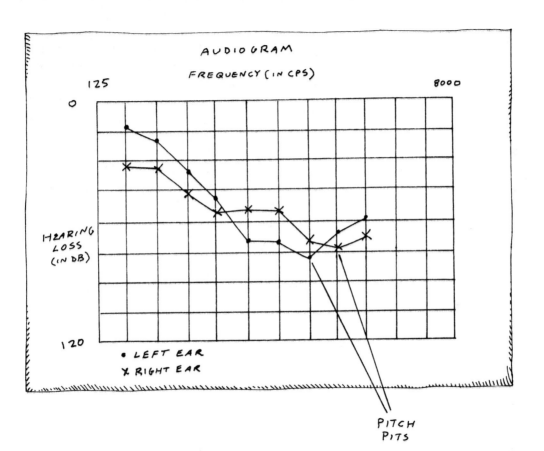

AUDIOGRAM

FREQUENCY (IN CPS)

125   8000

0

HEARING
LOSS
(IN DB)

120

• LEFT EAR
✗ RIGHT EAR

PITCH
PITS

87

POSTNIKS
(POST niks)

n. **DEAFIES** who were born hearing and dumb, but by the age of two, become deaf and babbling.

PRENIKS
(PREE niks)

n. **DEAFORMED DEAFIES**; i.e. **DEAFIES** who don't acquire speech in the same way as **HEARIES** do.

PROBOSCISHADOW
(pro BOS ki shah dow)

n. The darkened area immediately below the nose which results when one stands directly below a bright light.

PSEUDOKNOB
(SOO doh nob)

v. To pretend to turn on the headphones or hearing aid, usually to deceive schoolteachers or mothers.

QUEUEVASION
(KEW vay shun)

n. A short-cut tactic cleverly employed by some **DEAFIES** who simply go to the front of a long line of people to explain they are deaf and therefore cannot hear anything.

QUIETBUSTERS
(KWY et bus ters)

n. Those hard-core **DEAFIES** who are notorious for creating all kinds of noise anywhere.

RADARSCAN

(RAY dar skan)

v. To look around oneself to make sure there are no **OOPSTACLES** or others trying to get one's attention.

REARSNIFFING

(REER snif fing)

n. The canine-like routine that takes place only on the streets, when a deaf driver spots a familiar-looking bumper decal (such as "Gallaudet University Parking Permit") on a car ahead of him, and he then sneaks up from behind and peeks in the car to see if he recognizes the driver.

RETRO-STROLL

(RE troh strohl)

n. A common sidewalk phenomenon in which two walking **DEAFIES** continually step back to get a better view of the other's signs and lips.

REVODAMN
(RE voh DAM)

n. A silly situation where one puts the phone in the reverse order on the telephone modem of the TDD.

RIPOSTARE
(ri POH stayr)

n. The same rude stare which **DEAFIES** return to that of **HEARIES**.

RIPPLATTENTAP
(ripl uh TEN tap)

v. To **ATTENTAP** each other in a deaf audience to pay attention to the speaker before he begins.

ROOMBROOM
(room broom)

v. To search for a **DEAFIE** in a large studio that has a lot of high partition walls.

SCHIZOMORPHOSIS
(SKIZ uh MOR foh sis)

n. The instantaneous transformation which a **DEAFIE** undergoes twice every working day at his hearing company's revolving doors: once in the morning when walking in and again in the evening when rushing out to join other roaming **DEAFIES**.

SHAKESPEARIGN
(shayk SPIR yn)

v. To sign or not to sign. (This troubling dilemma often afflicts oralists.)

SHUNT-EYE
(SHUNT y)

n. An evasive eye movement used to break off or to avoid visual contact.

SIGNBLAST RADIUS

(syn blast RAY dee us)

n. The area in front of a **DEAFIE** sitting at a table from which all the drinking glasses have been evacuated.

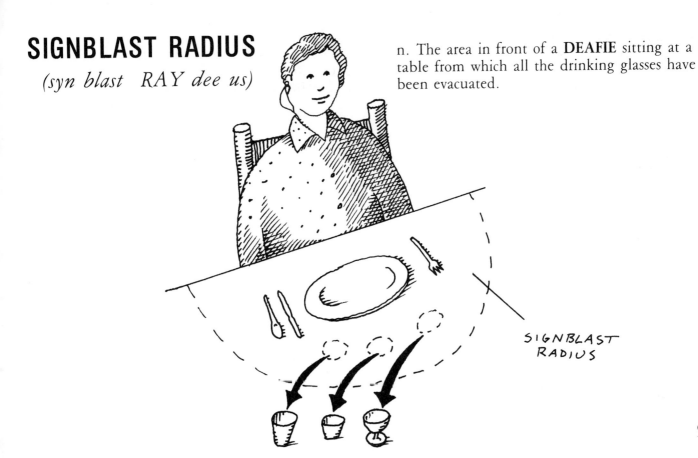

SIGNBLAST RADIUS

93

SIGNFERENCE
(SYN fer ens)

n. Disruption in communication usually caused by **HEARIES** ineptly **COMMUNAVIGATING** a herd of **DEAFIES**.

SIGNICIDE
(SYN uh syd)

n. The act of interrupting a signer to correct a sign.

SIGNITION
(syn ISH un)

n. Any heated argument in rapid-fire manual communication.

SIGNLETS
(SYN lits)

n. Words pertaining to the world of the deaf that are not in the dictionary but should be.

SIGNORAMUS
(sig nuh RAY mus)

n. A person who mistakenly thinks he knows how to sign.

SIGNUS INTERRUPTUS
(SYN us   IN ter RUP tus)

n. The sudden halt in a deep conversation between two **DEAFIES** caused by a **HEARIE** inadvertently walking in between. (Also known as **INTERRUPTED INTERCOURSE**.)

SITRAIGHTINE
(SIT ray tyn)

v. To sit down facing each other to establish a **VISUALINE**.

SLASHOICES
(SLASH oy suz)

n. Those little V/T's found beside the telephone numbers in TDD directories.

SLUNKOIN
(SLUNK koyn)

n. Any coin that has slipped through a hole in the pocket of a walking **DEAFIE**'s pants and is left behind on the floor.

SNAFU (SITES' NAMES ALL FOULED UP)

(sna FEW)

n. Extremely confusing situation brought about by an announcement over a loudspeaker that the scheduled destinations have been changed, all unknown to the deaf traveler.

SOFT-OF-DEAF

(SOFT of def)

adj. Hard-of-hearing; unable to perceive some sounds. (Compare with **HARD-OF-DEAF**.)

SOLARM

(SOH larm)

n. Makeshift alarm system, in which a **DEAFIE** is awakened by a bright window, its curtains purposely left undrawn. Highly unreliable during the rainy season.

97

SPASTISIGN
(SPAS ti syn)

v. To put together signs in a very awkward manner.

SPLING
(spling)

v. Abbreviated finger-spelling, in which some letters are omitted.

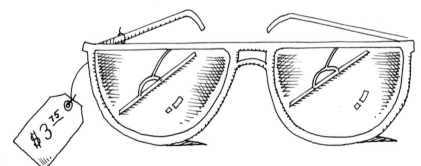

$3^{75}

SPROXIMITES
(SPROHKS i myts)

n. The little wet flecks of spittle a **DEAFIE** often gets on the face from an **IDIOTSPRAYER**.

SQUIMOSIS
(skwi MOH sis)

n. A paralyzing condition some **DEAFIES** experience when facing a crowd of both **HEARIES** and **DEAFIES**.

STARESTABBED
(STAYR stabd)

adj. Experiencing the queasy feeling that a million eyes are on one's back while sitting with an interpreter out in front of a huge audience.

STOMPOPHOBIA
(STOMP oh FOH bee uh)

n. The fear some **DEAFIES** have of somebody banging on the floor (with feet) or on the table (with hands) right behind them to get their attention.

STROBBOCK
(STROHB bok)

n. A nauseating feeling a **DEAFIE** gets after being awakened from deep sleep by a flashing strobe light, especially in dormitories at deaf colleges.

STRUCTRODUCE
(struk truh DOOS)

v. To introduce a **DEAFIE** by saying "First" and "Last" before spelling out the first name and last name respectively, and then to add where he went to school.

SUBTITLE SUBTLETY
(SUB tyt ul SUT ul tee)

n. An annoying phenomenon in TV-watching in which the captions do not reflect everything the actors say.

SUPERCHAT

(SOO per chat)

v. To carry on a leisurely conversation through the huge storefront window at a supermarket.

SYGNOPHANT
(SYN uh funt)

n. A person who signs to flatter or to impress **DEAFIES**.

SYNCHECK
(SYN chek)

v. To pause in an **INTERPRIVY** now and then to maintain the appearance of faithfully interpreting the boring speaker.

TABLE-TAP
(TAY bul tap)

v. To get a **DEAFIE**'s attention by pounding on the table.

TACTILE TACTIC
(TAK tul   TAK tik)

n. The method widely used by **DEAFIES** where a household appliance or a machine is touched manually to determine whether it is running or not.

TAPCRATERS

(TAP kray ters)

n. Sore bruises or marks found on the sides of **DEAFIES'** arms, usually caused by **UNCONTACTFUL ATTENTAPPERS**.

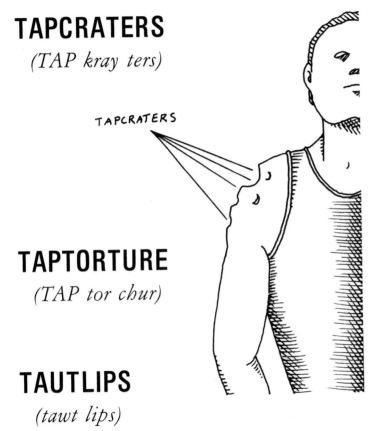

TAPCRATERS

TAPTORTURE

(TAP tor chur)

adj. A maddening state a **DEAFIE** finds himself in whenever a **HEARIE** taps rhythmically on the table or on the floor.

TAUTLIPS

(tawt lips)

n. Lips that are tense, thin, and/or small, which makes lipreading difficult. Often leads to **OPHTHALMATIGUE**.

TELL-TAIL
(TEL tayl)

n. That portion of the hearing-aid cord that sticks out from under the ear for all to see.

TENNIS NECK
(TEN nis nek)

n. A minor ailment that afflicts **DEAFIES**, usually caused by a prolonged attempt to follow the conversation between two people sitting at opposite ends of a long table.

TOLLBLAST
(tol blast)

n. Noise explosion often experienced by highway tollbooth operators when deaf drivers forget to turn their blaring radios down.

TONEWALLING
(TOHN wal ing)

v. Refusing to "listen" by closing one's eyes.

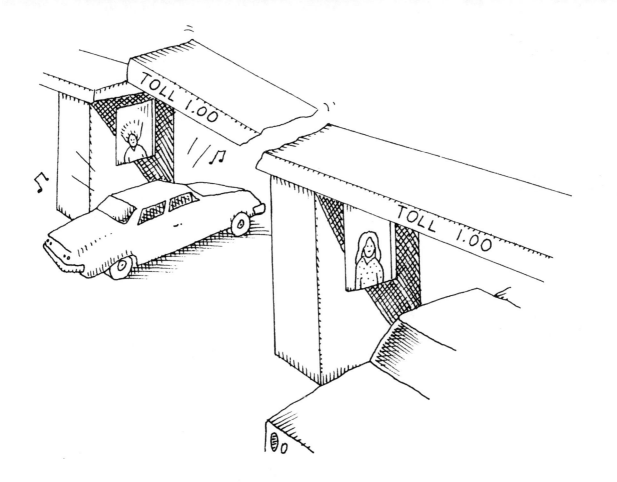

TORTURANCE
(TOR chur ans)

n. An uncomfortable situation where a **DEAFIE** finds himself sitting in the middle of an audience with no interpreter around to interpret a two-hour long lecture.

TOTALISTS
(TOH tahl ists)

n. **DEAFIES** who are both oral and manual. (Not to be confused with **HEARIES** who total their cars.)

TOUCH-TONE
(TUCH tohn)

v. To place one's hand and fingers directly over the loudspeaker so as to appreciate the music.

TRANSVESTWATTLE
(TRANS ves TWAT ul)

v. To "voice" for a **DEAFIE** of the opposite sex on telephone.

TWILIGHT TALK
(TWY lyt tawk)

n. Hurried signed conversation between sunset and total darkness.

UNCONTACTFUL
(UN kon TAKT ful)

adj. Unnecessarily rough in **ATTENTAPPING**.

VACSUCKER

(VAK suk er)

n. A **DEAFIE** who continues vacuuming after the plug is inadvertantly pulled out of its socket.

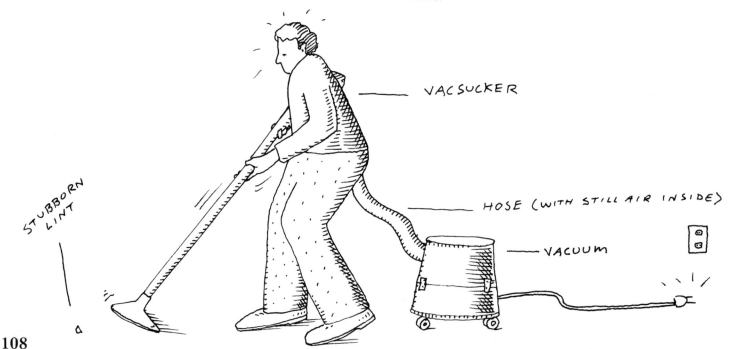

STUBBORN LINT

VACSUCKER

HOSE (WITH STILL AIR INSIDE)

VACUUM

VARM
(varm)

n. The warm, nice feeling of relief when the earmold is taken out of the ear.

VEEROLOGY
(VEER oh luh jee)

n. The science and art of how to guide **DEAFIES** into new positions and directions. Widely used by Vocational Rehabilitation (VR) counselors.

VEESTUCK
(VEE stuk)

n. One of many communication games **DEAFIES** play, in which they fork the "V" sign to their own throat and say loudly (or quietly) "STUCK!" to a victim who is momentarily at a loss for a verbal comeback.

VIBRACATCHA

(VY bra KAT cha)

n. Any vibration that automatically draws the attention of a **DEAFIE**.

VISUALINE

(VIZH yew uh lyn)

n. Clear, unobstructed view between two or more **DEAFIES** - vital for face-to-face communication.

VISUCLAP

(VIZH yew klap)

v. To applaud by waving handkerchiefs or napkins, especially at **DEAFIE** reception dinners or banquets.

WAVILY

(WAY vuh lee)

v. To say farewell with the "I love you" hand sign (three fingers spelling I, L, and Y simultaneously).

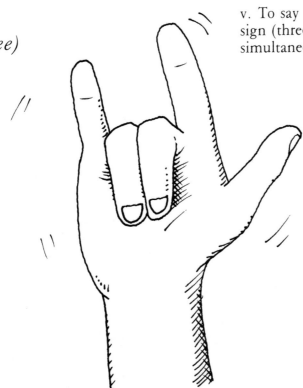

WAXBLOW
(WAKS bloh)

v. To clean out the channel in the earmold by blowing.

WHISPIGN
(WHIS pyn)

v. To sign softly.

WITORT
(wi TORT)

v. To retort wittily in the act of **MYTHICIDE**. Examples: ''Can you write?'' in response to ''Can you read?'' and ''Something'' to ''Are you deaf or something?''

WONG 'N' NUMB
(WONG an NUM)

adj. Feeling helpless with a telephone dangling from one's hand after a **HEARIE** hangs up without recognizing the beeping sounds created by one's teletype.

WUNNING
(WUN ning)

n. Running or dripping water in the sink or shower left unattended by a **DEAFIE**.

XAGGIES
(ZAG jeez)

n. (TDD communication) Misspelled GA's and SK's.

YAPYAKYAWK
(YAP yak yawk)

v. (In conversation) To nod one's head affirmatively, repeatedly, and synchronously with the "Y" sign.

ZESTROOL
(ZEST rool)

v. To behave in a silly manner so as to obtain temporary relief or enjoyment while in a group of boring **HEARIES**.

113

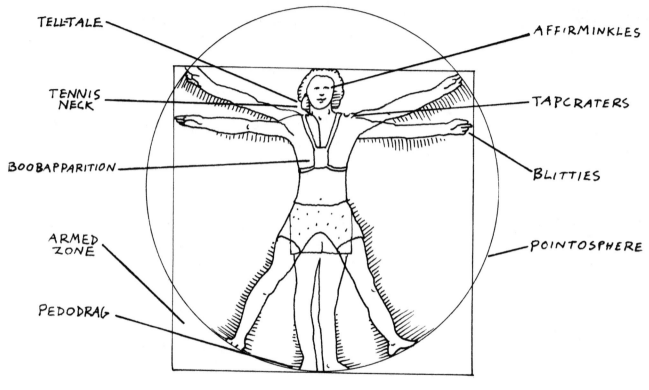

TELLTALE

AFFIRMINKLES

TENNIS NECK

TAPCRATERS

BOOBAPPARITION

BLITTIES

ARMED ZONE

POINTOSPHERE

PEDODRAG

114

DEAFIE

Official SIGNLETS Entry Form

Dear Ken:

Here's a new **SIGNLET** I've just invented. I understand that submission of this **SIGNLET** constitutes my permission for it to be published in any sequels and, if it is accepted, I will receive a free copy of the sequel.

SIGNLET: _____

DEAFINITION: _____

_____

_____

Sincerely,

Name: _____

Street: _____

City, State, Zip: _____

DiKen Products
9201 Long Branch Parkway
Silver Spring, Maryland 20901

DEAFinitions Posters

Black on White

"Deaf...is probably one of the most colorful words in the English language...."

That's how the poster begins. And then, it delves further into the word "deaf" and brings out all its nuances. As its title suggests, deaf's "DEAFinitions" are listed—touching just about everything the word implies: deafness, deaf people, deaf talk, deaf world, hearing people, hearing talk, and even a deaf dog!

Delightfully humorous, with 50 examples to make your world go 'round!

Makes a nice picture as well as a nice gift.

$6.00 each poster for **16" by 20"**; $7.50 each for **24" by 36"**
(Postage & Shipping: $1.50, Maryland Residents: add 5% Sales Tax)

DiKen Products, 9201 Long Branch Parkway, Silver Spring, Maryland 20901

"DEAFinitions" - Copyright 1986 by Kenneth P. Glickman

FOSSILLOTES

SIGNLETS WORKSHEET